THE ALL NEW STYLE OF MAGAZINE-BOOKS

SDM LIVE®

www.SDMLIVE.com

MP

MOCY PUBLISHING
WWW.MOCYPUBLISHING.COM

Printed by CreateSpace, An Amazon.com Company

REAL MUSIC. REAL ENTERTAINMENT.®

SDM LIVE

ISSUE 12

Also
PHILLY FAL
7MILE
RADIO
NO'EL
SNYDER
SARAH
APPLEB
LASURIA
"KANDI"
ALLMAN

NEW
KING DILLON
EXCLUSIVE P DOT

CHARLIE B. KEYZ
PUTTING IN MAJOR
LEGWORK IN THE
INDUSTRY

TOYSOULJA
LAGOON
THE NEWEST
MEMBER OF
TEAM MONEY
HUNGRY

WWW.SDMLIVE.COM

SDM LIVE®

EDITOR-IN-CHIEF
D. "Casino" Bailey
casino@sdmlive.com

EDITORIAL DIRECTOR
Sheree Cranford
sheree@sdmlive.com

GRAPHIC/WEB DESIGNER
D. "Casino" Bailey
casino@sdmlive.com

ACCOUNT EXECUTIVE
Frank Harvest Jr.
frank@sdmlive.com

PHOTOGRAPHERS
Anterlon Terrell Fritz
Treagen Colston
Terance Drake

CONTRIBUTORS
April Smiley
Courtney Benjamin

COPY ORDERS & ADVERTISING OFFICE
Send Money Order or Check to:
Mocy Publishing
P.O. Box 35195
Detroit, Michigan 48235
(586) 646-8505
advertise@sdmlive.com

Copy Order Item
SDM Live Magazine Issue #14
S&H Plus Retail Price - $9.99 per copy

WWW.SDMLIVE.COM

Printed by CreateSpace, An Amazon.com Company

MP
MOCY PUBLISHING

REAL MUSIC. REAL ENTERTAINMENT.®
SDM LIVE
ISSUE #14

Also
KIKI
MALIKA
BIG PAPA
MOOD
UNTAMED
LE'LAN

NEW
3XOTIC
THE NEW FACE OF BEAUTY & MUSIC

LYRICQ
A TRIO BRINGING BACK THE ESSENCE OF A MUSIC GROUP

PAULY BRONSON
GETTING READY TO MAKE A COMEBACK
#TRIPLEDOUBLE

WWW.SDMLIVE.COM

CONTENTS

1

Audio-Technica - Professional Turntable - Silver
$249.99
www.bestbuy.com

2

Polk Audio - 5-1/4" Bookshelf Speakers - Pair - Black
$99.98
www.bestbuy.com

3

HP - Spectre x360 2-in-1 15.6" 4K Ultra HD Touch-Screen Laptop - Intel Core i7 - 16GB Memory - 256GB Solid State Drive - Natural Silver
$1079.99
www.bestbuy.com

Clowning The Potus

RAPPER AND POLITICAL ACTIVIST SNOOP DOGG MAKES A BIG STATEMENT WITH THE VISUALS IN HIS LATEST MUSIC VIDEO .

by Cheraee C.

Hip Hop legend Snoop Dogg recently released a controversial music video firing shots at our POTUS Donald Trump. The video also shows a white man getting shot by a white cop paying homage to all the lives that have been taken by white police officials. Some people feel like Snoop Dogg is disrespecting our POTUS, but I salute him. I rather watch a video about real life issues then watch musicians throwing fake money and driving rental cars .Hip-Hop has always been a political and subliminal form of music.

If anybody is in the wrong it's Donald Trump for responding or caring about Snoop Dogg's video. Trump shouldn't have time to have Twitter fingers or stalk the internet to see who's criticizing him. Concrete on America Trump!

Around the Way Girl

FROM DC TO HOLLYWOOD TARAJI P. HENSON WRITES A CLASSIC MEMOIR EXPLAINING HER DRIVE AND AMBITION TO SUCCESS.

by Cheraee C.

More and more celebrities are writing memoirs detailing their life stories. You'll be surprised what experiences celebrities faced before they became famous and after the fame. Some popular movies Taraji has starred in include

Baby Boy, Hustle and Flow, No Good Deed, Hidden Figures, the TV Series Empire, and many others.

Actress Taraji P. Henson reveals how she struck stardom from her hometown DC to Hollywood, college experiences from Harvard University, industry experiences being a black author, and many more. Taraji is just another talented black woman in pursuit of her dreams despite the glisten and red carpets.

If you love memoirs this book is definitely a must read.

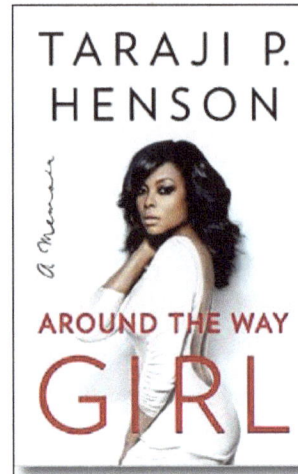

Around the Way Girl: A Memoir
By Taraji P. Henson

Available from Amazon.com and other online stores

COMING SOON!!!

A BOOK OF SHORT STORIES & POETRY

Brown Paper Suga

forwarded by
Cheraee C.

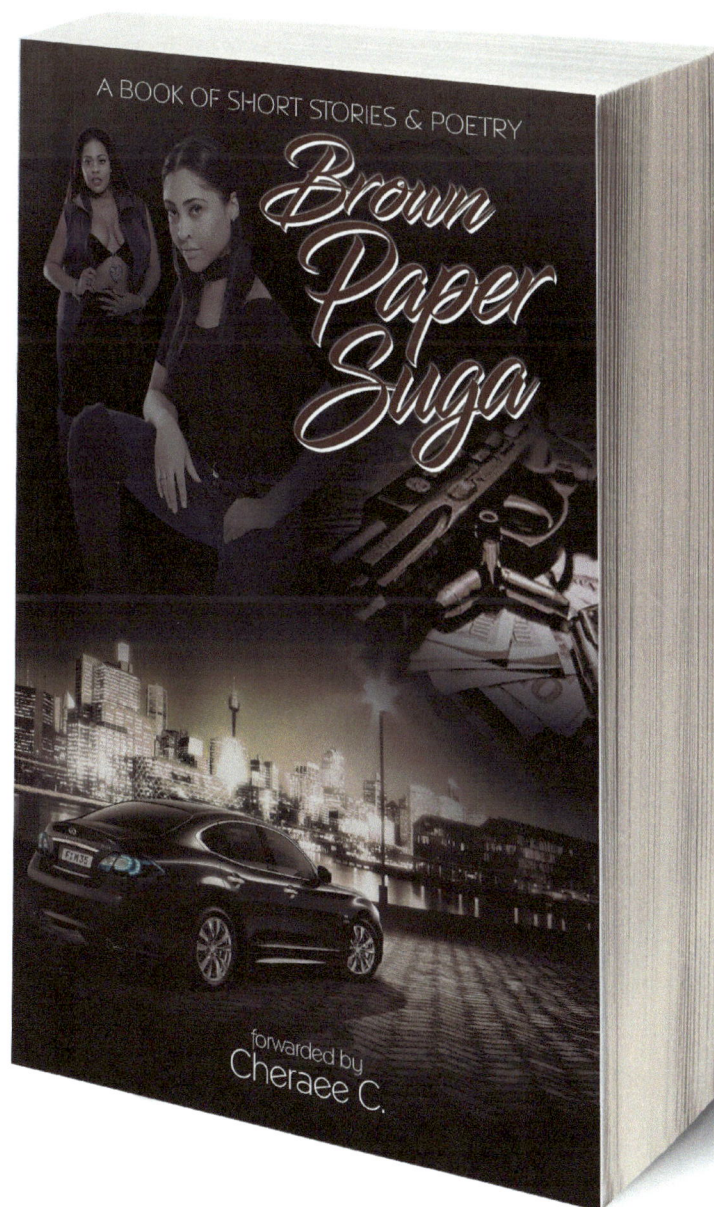

Brown Paper Suga
By Cheraee C.

Blending Three Melodies

COLETTE, ANGELO, AND PROLYPIC THE PROFESSIONAL MAKEING THE BLENDED SENSATION OF SOUND CALLED LYRICQ.

by Cheraee C.

Q. Who are the members in Lyricq and how did you guys meet each other?

A. The Hip-Hop & R&B collective Lyricq consists of lead vocalist and songwriter Colette Treece, songwriter and rapper Angelo Alford, and producer/songwriter Prolyphic The Professional. The group was formed as Prolyphic The Professional met Colette Treece through a high school friend, and met Angelo Alford through a high school friend and rap artist C Dell.

Q. What made you guys form a music group and what is each individual's musical talent?

A. The group is a perfect combination of smooth instrumental beds provided by Prolyphic, complimented by the easy listening vocal talent of Colette and the dynamic songwriting provided by Angelo Alford. The group came together through writing sessions and discovering each person's strength and the natural blend of each one's talent. Formed in 2014, the early days were rough in terms of discovering what works best for all members, however we have now gelled quite easily and know what sounds brings out the best in all of us.

Q. What challenges have you guys faced so far being a music group? Have you changed your name or lost any members at any certain point?

A. The group has undergone one name change, going to Lyricq from The Link. Thus far, the biggest challenge has been finding the perfect or niche audience in the today's music landscape as everything seems to be here today gone tomorrow and all about the party and nightlife. We like to consider our music as the perfect soundtrack for Sunday through Thursday, with quaint, laid back through provoking sounds. The group has undergone a change from 4 members to 3, as will be evident on the upcoming project titled "Imagine It's Yesterday."

Q. How did you guys meet DJ Hollyhood and become apart of his mixtape project?

A. We met DJ Hollyhood through rap artist C Dell and have formed a relationship beginning several years ago. Prolyphic & Angelo have also worked with fellow artist Cezar The Gladiator who has ties to DJ Hollyhood. Prolyphic was approached by DJ Hollyhood to be a part of his Romeo Must Die mixtape, as well as hosting it on the website www. MusicByPro.com for distribution. www.MusicByPro.com has also previously played host to another project of DJ Holly-

hood's, titled Christmas Day Massacre.

Q. If it's any group that you guys can compare yourself too new or old who would it be and why?

A. The group can be compared to The Fugees, in make up only, as it contains a female lead, in house producer/rapper and a second male songwriter/rapper. However, Lyricq's sound and message does differ, taking more of a back and forth approach between 90's hip-hop & R&B beats to today's current trap sound and socially conscious messages mixed with some playful topics and uneasy subject matter. We're also always looking to work with any other artists and possibly making group additions.

Q. What music/project are you guys currently working on now?

A. Lyricq is currently working on its sophomore release, titled "Imagine It's Yesterday." The title suggests thinking back to the best moment(s) in your life and/or being the best version of yourself and moving forward with that attitude or feeling. The albums tracks are a mix of upbeat, bouncy records and laid back lounge/chill vibes. Subject matter for the album covers police brutality, relationships, bragging rights and more. The album is slated to be released Spring 2017 and will be available in all digital music stores as well as LyricqMusic.com & MusicByPro.com.

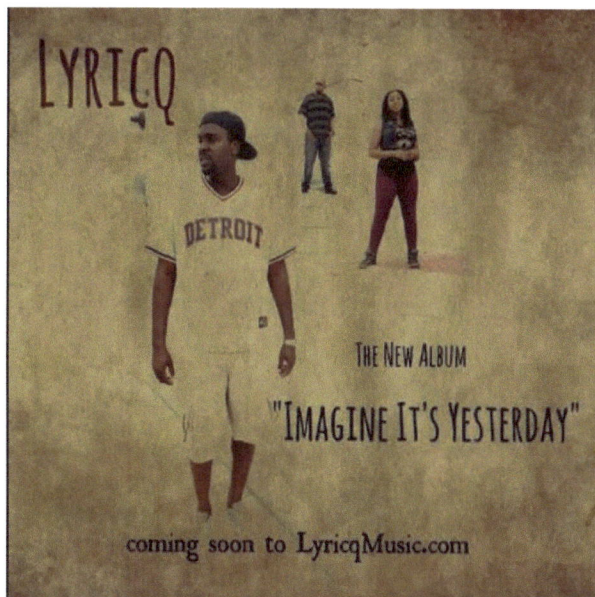

LYRICQ

THE NEW ALBUM

"IMAGINE IT'S YESTERDAY"

coming soon to LyricqMusic.com

Fiery New Voice

TEAM MONEY HUNGRY'S NEWEST R&B VOICE KIKI WATERS BRINGS HER VOCAL, DANCE, AND STAGE PRESENCE SKILLS TO THE GROUP

by Cheraee C.

Q. What made you want to become a part of Team Money Hungry?

A. TMH just had an undeniable energy about their performance and their management does such a great job promoting that I knew I would be winning to be a part of TMH. The icing on the cake was that we're already affiliated through family so it wasn't like they were taking on a complete stranger.

Q. As a songwriter how do you feel about artists who don't write their own music?

A. I feel like writing your own music is the purest way to truly express exactly what you mean. Only you can make your song have understanding and meaning.

Q. If you couldn't do music what would you do to replace it?

A. Gosh, that's a hard one. I would dance. That's like my next passion.

Q. Do you feel like you gotta migrate from Michigan to be successful?

A. No I came up in places like Star Factory Artist Development center right here in MI that hones each individual's talent and presses them to be better. It's all about resources and chance.

Q. What is the craziest experience you've had so far in the music industry?

A. Being robbed fo fake showcases.

Gwap Game

RAP ARTIST UNTAMED IS A NEW COLLABORATIVE TO THE GROWING DETROIT SQUAD KNOWN AS TEAM MONEY HUNGRY

by: Cheraee C.

Q. What were you doing before you became a part of Team Money Hungry?

A. I was just voted into TMH the beginning of this month, but Gwap Game is something I started and fushed with TMH.

Q. What's Gwap Game and what did you have to do to get voted in?

A. Gwap Game is a group I started back in 2007. I lost a couple members, but gained who I needed to make us who we are as of 2017. To get voted into TMH you got to have talent and most of all ambition, but it's a team decision who's in and who's out.

Q. So are you apart of the group and a solo artist at the same time? Untamed? Gwap Game? TMH?

A. Yes and no. I am a solo artist so I have a couple solo mixtapes. Gwap Game is me, like I said I started it back in 2007 with "Cartier Los." He is no longer apart of it so I kept the name and added an abbreviation "G2" which is still Gwap Game. Then my brothers joined me and made it what it is today. TMH is a collective organization of individual artists that support one another.

Q. What motivated you to want to take your music more seriously?

A. What motivates my music is the fact that people really believe in me and believe in what I'm doing so that pushes me to do what I do. On top of that I just had my first son. He's four months so that's a whole other arrive.

Q. Who would you say is the greatest underground legend in the D and why?

A. I'm a be real. I don't really listen to many people, but for who I do listen to RIP to Blade Icewood and the reason why is because he opened a lot of doors for a lot of people coming up in Detroit. He set a way for young artists to make a way today.

Eccentrically Exotic

GET LOST IN 3XOTIC'S MUSIC BOX AS SHE REVEALS THE UNCUT DEFINITION OF BEING BOLDLY EXOTIC.

by Cheraee C.

Q. What is your favorite single on your new album and why?
A. My favorite single? I wish I did have a favorite single for this project. I'm actually proud to say I love each and every song equally. This album shows so much growth since my last one in 2014. It also shows a total different side of 3xotic. Hidd3n Colors tells a story of behind the scenes emotions that people didn't know. Situations people can relate to far as relationships, heartbreak, and regaining confidence to move forward with a fresh start at finding love.

Q. What's your zodiac sign and how do you think your sign affects your music?
A. I'm an Aries and my birthday is March 28th. . Aries, the fire sign... known to be passionate and bold natural leaders. I feel my sign affects the flow of my music in the passionate love making way. Most of my material shows me expressing that passionate side. I just do me; which has led me into creating my own lane that makes me stand out musically, even in my performances.

Q. What is your opinion of all the rap beef going on between Remy and Nicki Minaj?
A. Personally I feel like it's unnecessary. I feel, if most of us were only focused on our own crafts and come together to build instead of hate, comparing and trying to prove points; a lot of artists would be further then they are. I'm more of a Nicki supporter personally. I like the fact she semi took the higher route. As women we tend to already self hate and shame each other. I felt the whole "beef" and all the energy it took could've been focused on them coming together to create a stronger lane for the female hip hop community.

Q. It's no secret you are a sex symbol. Why are you so infatuated and open about sex?
A. It's not more so sex that I'm open about. It's the infatuation of love…and expressing everything inside of love; which also includes sex. lol.

Q. For those who want to know is 3xotic single or in a relationship?
A. I am currently single. I'm focusing on my craft, but I'm not opposed to dating.

Q. You are a very visual and opinionated person. When are you going to start your own podcast or radio show?
A. I've had a lot of people ask me. I am open to that but right now I actually like the "going live" on Facebook thing. I like people to be able to see and interact with me. See me dress up for themes and promote different business and events. Since I have been doing Facebook Live; my fan base has risen even more. I

3xotic's Box

3xoticmusic.com

have people requesting me to talk and discuss certain topics. We have fun! I don't think it wouldn't be the same if I was on the radio or behind the scenes. I love to see the love LIVE!

Q. Your sound and range is different from most female R&B artists. Do you feel like female artists are intimidated by you and your confidence?

A. I actually get a lot of love and admiration. I'm not sure if it's fake, but love is still shown. I'm the type of artist that still goes out and supports all the females. I give advice when asked and help as many female artists develop their craft as much as I can. I'm all about building confidence and guiding people in the right direction. So I would hope not.

Q. Since you represent being exotic. What is the most exotic thing you would do in a music video?

A. As you know Exotic means "strangely beautiful, not of the ordinary". I've raised the bar a little with my "Rain " video showing more skin than usual. For me to be plus size, you wouldn't expect me to be comfortable showing my body in a sexual way. I'm not opposed to anything in my videos; as long as it fits my character and the messages I like to portray.

SHADY LEGENDS

RICK ROSS'S SHADE IS REAL ON BIRDMAN ABOUT SHADY BUSINESS.

by Semaja Turner

Rick Ross is taking his grief and beef to the streets with some new, tell all music. His new track "Idols Become Rivals" is informing the industry facts about the real Birdman. The Birdman behind closed doors may not be as bossy or flossy as we thought he was. Ross claims that Birdman has stolen artists publishing earnings, he owes some music producers, he played DJ Khaled, and he ultimately played Lil Wayne.

This track might drag Birdman back to the studio so he can tell his side of story. The Nicki and Remy beef will no longer matter once these two go at it. Too many legends can speak on Birdman, Cash Money, and Lil Wayne.

SDM LIVE®

Face The Music

UPON RELEASING HIS FIRST EP, HE OVERCOMES HIS BIGGEST BATTLE OF PROCRASTINATION, THE FIRST BIG STEP FOR BIG PAPA MOOD.

Q. Do you think a lot of underground artists suffer from life and procrastination?

A.I do, I think we all do at the some point in our lives. Procrastination is something as artists or an average Joes we suffer from. I feel like with underground artists, it has a lot to do with wanting to get the sound right, not being sure if it's good enough. Wondering if it's "mainstream" as far as life is concerned. You could be trying to spend some money on studio time and you need money for rent, just life lol.

Q. When and what is your most creative element for making music?

A. I have been making music for fun or a hobby since about 2009. I developed a weird love for it and depending on my mood my beats would reflect it. It was a way for me to get my feelings out. As of recently it would have to be my daughter Marley, she's my motivation, she's what got and keeps the fire burning.

Q. Why did your name change from just Moody to Papa Mood?

A. Moody, lol yeah like I said, it depended on my mood that determined what type of music I made and me being me I needed a deeper meaning and it's an acronym for Man of ordinary dreams and if you ask about the y is, why not? The name change organically, came once Marley was born. Friends instantly start calling me Papa Mood so I coined it as my name. It was a real reflection of me.

Q. It's hard getting people to invest in you. What made your girlfriend want to invest in your talents?

A. I wouldn't say so because real recognize real. I would meet people, we would work consistently for a while and ultimately it was just me and my procrastination that caused a lot of people to be reluctant to want to work with me. She saw my love for the music and saw me holding myself back. She saw what I would be if I stopped bullshittin.

Q. Branding and networking are important methods for being industrious. Do you think you're better at branding and working or both?

A. I would say networking, branding not so much.

When it comes to people, idk I'm big on vibes you know. I can feel someone's energy and know and they know I'm a genuine dude, and now that I'm serious about my business.

Q. What inspired the title of your new EP you recently released? Why did you choose to release your EP on Valentine's Day?

A. I was Bullshittin is like a self titled album because I was and have been bullshittin. People know I made music and I never had anything to show for it. I knew it was time to stop bullshittin and let the world know.

Masterminding Greatness

THE TOP SHELF ARTIST PAULY BRONSON IS NOT LEAVING
2017 WITHOUT A BANG AND DROPPING NEW MUSIC.

by Cheraee C.

Q. How long have you been in the industry and what is
Top Shelf Entertainment?

A. Officially since 2005. Top Shelf is a entertainment
company that includes music and film. Created by
myself and the labels namesake Top Shelf who is also
responsible for Premium Taste Catering, one of the more
popular catering companies in Detroit.

Q. What is the craziest experience you've ever had in a
recording studio?

.A. I can't get to specific but I'll say sex and just leave it at
that! Lol!

Q. Do you feel like it's more idols or rivals in the industry and why?

A. I'd say a bit of both. But once you become a revered
artist you're definitely going to encounter plenty rivals.
Hip Hop is based in competition.

Q. Name one song of yours you feel like deserves a music award and why?

A. "Get Cha Money Up" off Campaign Trail 2: The
primaries. This song took me to A3C, SXSW(South by
southwest) and 4 other states!!! It's a song that gets the
crowd involved, and it's my most popular song to date.

Q. Have you ever taken a break from the music industry
and if so why?

A. Actually yes, I've been on a bit of a hiatus for the last
2-3 years. I did a couple features, but I haven't released
no single, mixtape, or album. Three people extremely
close to me passed away and it affected me immensely.
Now I'm using it as the driving force for my return!!!

Q. Do you have a specific number or status that you are
trying to reach in the next few years?

A. Absolutely!!! You have to set goals to keep the focus.
With that being said I plan on dropping two mixtapes
and an album this year. Within a year I plan on being
mentioned with the best artists in Detroit!!!!

TOP 10 CHARTS

TOP 10 DIGITAL SINGLES AND ALBUMS
APRIL 1, 2017

TOP 10 CHARTS

FUTURE "SUPER TRAPPER," FEATURING CEE-LO GREEN AND TONE TRUMP.

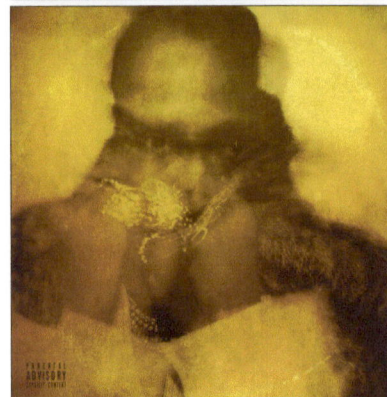

TOP 10 SINGLES
CHART OF THE MONTH

No.	Artist - Song Title
1	FUTURE - MASK OFF
2	KHALID - LOCATIONS
3	CHILDISH GAMBINO - REDBONE
4	MACHINE GUN KELLY - BAD THINGS
5	MIGOS - BAD AND BOUJEE
6	JP ONE - MILLION
7	YOUNG M.A. - OOOUUU
8	RIHANNA - LOVE ON THE BRAIN
9	BIG SEAN - BOUNCE BACK
10	J. COLE - DEJA VU

TOP 10 ALBUMS
CHART OF THE MONTH

No.	Artist - Album Title
1	FUTURE - FUTURE
2	KHALID - AMERICAN TEEN
3	J COLE - FOR YOUR EYES ONLY
4	KEHLANI - SWEETSEXTSAVAGE
5	BIG SEAN - I DECIDED
6	GUCCI MANE - THE RETURN OF EAST ATLANTA SANTA
7	THE WEEKND - STARBOY
8	MIGOS - CULTURE
9	RAE SREMMURD - SREMMLIFE 2
10	LIL UZI VERT - LIL UZI VERT VS. THE WORLD

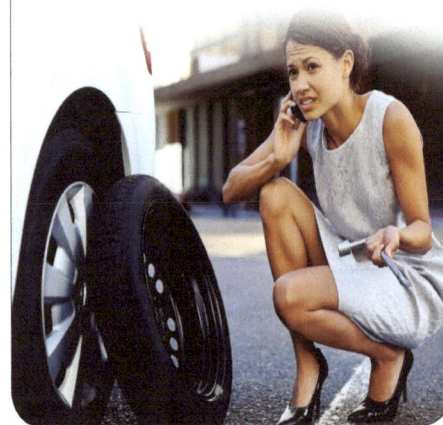

Romeo Must Die
ARTIST: DJ Hollyhood
RATING: 5

DJ HollyHood introduced a carnal, erotic, and lustful 17 Track, RnB Mixtape titled "Romeo Must Die". The Young DJ from Detroit, MI wanted to drop a R&B project on Valentine's Day. Reasons behind the title, it seems like we're living in the era where everyone is single and people are just looking for quick, sexual encounters, hookups. So he felt as if the artist and himself should kill Romeo metaphorically on Valentine's Day. It's great to hear something different from a DJ who's from Detroit to release a full hour of RnB music using all local artist in the city of Detroit. Dj Hollyhood wanted to do something different and I had to think to myself, when was the last time a Detroit DJ made a R&B mixtape. The Production came with low tempo beats with vibrant, gently laced soft vocals. Tracks like "Naked" by Shawny Marie, "Come Over" by ATM and "Temptation" by Rich Andrews immediately caught my attention, fist five seconds into the tracks. So many talented artist in the City of Detroit, shout to the artists, ATM, Rich Andrews, Rail Fresh, Malik's Jones, Nashad Davis, Cien Tell, Shawny Marie, Frank Fisher, Lyricq, Cezar, Pauly Bronson, MC. Beezy and 3xotic, keep making great music! "Romeo Must Die", is definitely the ultimate compilation for 2017 when it comes to RnB music in Detroit! Check out DJ Hollyhood's on Spotify!

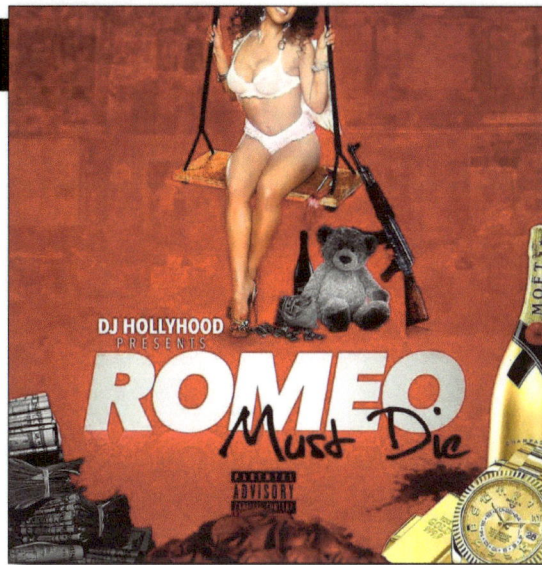

I Was Bullshittin
ARTIST: Big Papa Mood
RATING: 4

Throughout an entire week on Instagram, I occasionally found myself glancing at photo of this cover art that displayed a countdown. With this countdown came a young male, knocking on the door in The Heidelberg Project, with a beat machine behind his back. Curiosity took me to reach out to the 26 year old music artist from Detroit, MI to obtain more insight on his upcoming EP, "I Was Bullshittin". Becoming a father just six months ago, welcoming a baby girl into this world, Papa Mood decides it's time to buckle down, handle business with his new, acquired inspiration to release his highly anticipated EP. The "I Was Bullshittin'" EP outlines the narrative of a producer that struggles with procrastination by hoarding the beats that he creates; never releasing music, but being known for making the music. Papa Mood's EP came with a wide variety of different melodies and sounds. From mellow jazz to raunchy head nodders, this eclectic production done by David Sanya, Cash Money AP, Gambi, Taz Taylor, and Ayodlo with Features that intermix from Chadroto and the hip hop group "Bad Trip" that consist of Kris Harris & P. Rich. Tracks like "Cream" and "Back To It" come with mellow vibrations, focusing on an abundance of wealth throughout his journey as a music artist. Tracks like "Regular ", "If You Will", and the Hit Single, "Pull Up" brought so much color into the EP, Intermixing his personality gracefully with his lyrics. Really enjoyed the delivery on this EP, Definitely intrigued from beginning to the end, listened straight through. I know what good music sounds like and if you've been reading what I've been writing for this long, then you're going to enjoy this EP! "I Was Bullshittin" EP Drops February 14, 2017!

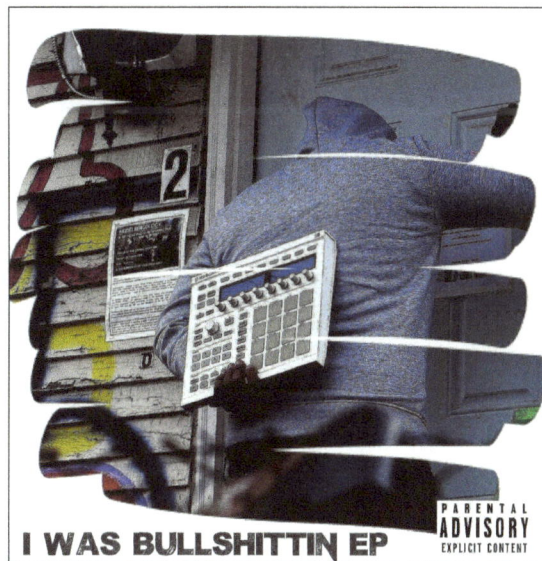

"Fuck A Clock, I'm Bout Punch My Boss, Tell That Nigga That I Need To Floss. You Got The Sauce, You Got That Juice, I Got That Seasoning. I Gotta Ball For My Daughter, That's My Reasoning"

HEELS &
SKILLZ

GINA SMILEZ
is a beautiful video
model from Detroit, MI.

instagram
@ginasmilez

Photography by
@barearmy

A Police officer in the movie True Religion from Detroit MI.

instagram
@therealbfocus

HEELS &
SKILLZ

Photography by
@barearmy

Cody-Brianna

Free-spirited Model,
Author, Makeup Artist,
Aspiring Singer and all
around entrepreneur.

instagram
@codybrianna

*Photography by
@terrancedrake*

Cheraee's Corner
WHAT'S UP WITH THE RISE OF INDUSTRY COPYCATS?
by **Cheraee C.**

It's a lot of multi-talented individuals in society who put in millions and years to be noteworthy moguls. Why do people think they can become moguls overnight after seeing someone else's empire? Why can't we stay in our own lanes until we have the knowledge, productivity, and power to be greater?

Why do we as individuals use our senses to backbite and copycat one another? Why can't we as individuals support and respect each other's brands?

We live in a small world so no point in trying to reuse or steal someone else"s clientale. When your brand and foundation is solid, nothing else matters not even copycats.

SDM LIVE®

NEXT 2 BLOW

MALIKA

Q. When and where did you have your first performance and describe that experience?

A. My first performance was in 1009 at the Kings and Queens Hall. It was a challenging experience because 2/4 members of my former singing group showed up.

Q. What former music group were you in and why did the group break up?

A. I was in three singing groups. In 1998 it was D-Town Cuties. From 1999-2001 it was Desire, and from 2009-2011 it was Fantasy D-Town Cuties. The members wouldn't get along. Desire disbanded from miscommunication amongst group and management. I left the group Fantasy to pursue a solo career. For some reason I always felt that I was more driven towards music. None of the other members til this day are pursuing music.

Q. Would you rather perform at an open mic night or perform at a showcase?

A. I would rather perform at a showcase. I like open mics, but a showcase is a great opportunity to get you into the music industry.

Q. What other projects have you been featured on besides DJ Hollyhood's Romie Must Die and how do you feel about your music career?

A. Romeo Must Die is actually my first featured project. I believe that my music career will be a huge success and I'm destined for greatness.

Q. How do you balance motherhood, songwriting, studio sessions, and etc?

A. That's easy for me because my kids come first, everything I do is for them. Writing is something I do everyday in my free time, and the studio is my second home when I'm not working.

Q. What is your current single and your next step in the music industry?

A. My current single is "In Love: which can be heard on the Romeo Must Die mixtape and my music page reverbnation.com/therealmalika. The next stop is continuing to create a buzz. In mid spring, I will be releasing another single so be on the lookout.

Q. Who is Le'Lan as an artist and what is your top goal to accomplish in the music industry?

A. I'm an R&B/Pop recording artist and a songwriter. Music is always something I have always had to grow up on. I love how music takes you through different moods. To make you remember different events in your life or to get you through a difficult time or just to make you feel good about yourself.

Q. What is the focal point of your music in the music industry?

A. I want to tell my story. I know everyone has a story to tell, but I want people to know my struggles. Then they can see how I got to where I'm at today, see how I handled things, and overcame them. Maybe the steps I took to handle different situations in my life will help another person going through the same thing.

Q. Give us some examples of a few personal struggles you sing about in your music?

A. Having personal roadblocks to keep me from my dream. How hard it is living from check to check and trying to do everything for my son and for myself. Losing my place living with other people tryna give my son a better life then what I lived growing up. Being in the foster care system. Just going through the system knowing that sometimes blood is not thicker than water. There are people willing to help you and take care of you even when your family didn't and didn't care too.

Q. Tell us about your first project and when you plan to release it?

A. I plan on dropping my first project in April called Domination. I have a few collabs with JP One, Gucci Rie, and a special collab with Chamere The Glam Princess of Kizzed clothing and cosmetics.

NEXT 2 BLOW

LE'LAN

SNAP SHOTS

Yasssssssss

Email Your Snap Shots to
snapshots@sdmlive.com

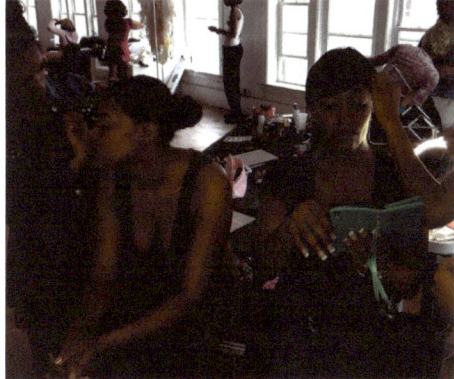

BASED ON A TRUE STORY
THE CHAPTER THAT CHANGED MY LIFE
BY MINYETTA NELSON-BAILEY
BASED ON A TRUE STORY
THE CHAPTER THAT CHANGED MY LIFE
BY MINYETTA NELSON-BAILEY
Available at amazon

DIRECTED BY CHERAEE C.
SOMETHING SHADY
WATCH THE SERIES PREMIERE
SUN 9P ET PT
SDM LIVE

5DS PRODUCTIONS®
THE PRINT MEDIA CENTER.

PRINT

GET 10% OFF WITH CODE: SAVE10OFF

DIGITAL & PRESS RUN PRICE LIST

BUSINESS CARD
2x3.5 INCHES

100	$10
500	$20
1000	$30
5000	$100
10000	$170

TRIFOLD BROCHURE
8.5x11 INCHES

250	$150
500	$180
1000	$230
5000	$350
10000	$680

POSTCARDS
4x6 INCHES

250	$50
500	$55
1000	$65
5000	$130
10000	$250

FLYERS - BROCHURES - BANNERS - BUSINESS CARDS - CD INSERTS
CALENDARS - EVENT TICKETS - POSTCARDS - POSTERS
YARD SIGNS - AND MUCH MORE

DIGITAL & PRESS RUN PRINTING

FAST TURN AROUND PRINTING

GET FREE SHIPPING ON ALL ORDERS

YOU SAVE MONEY WHEN YOU PRINT AT
WWW.THEPRINTMEDIACENTER.COM
24/7 ONLINE ORDERING. CALL US NOW 1.888.718.2999

COUPON CODE IS FOR A LIMITED TIME OFFER - FREE UPS SHIPPING ANYWHERE IN THE US

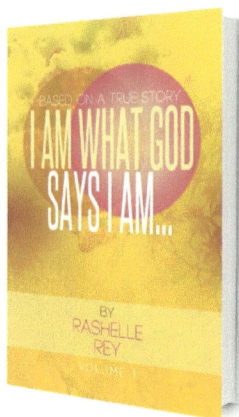

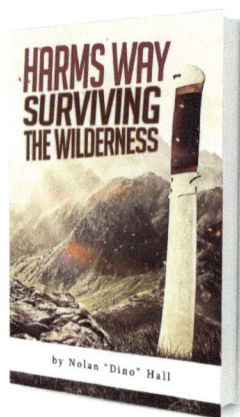

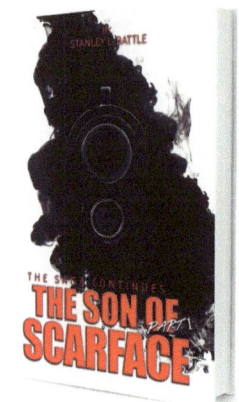

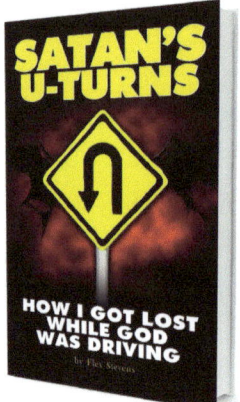

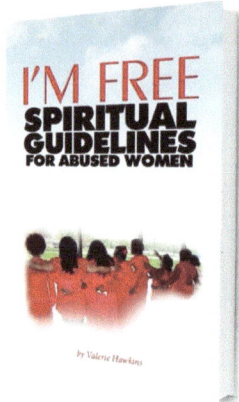

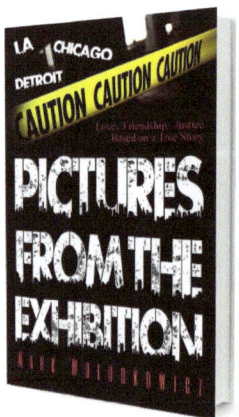

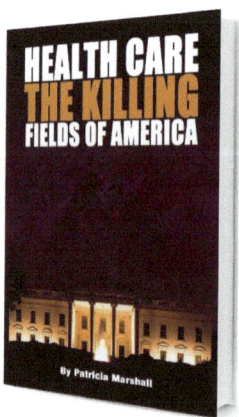

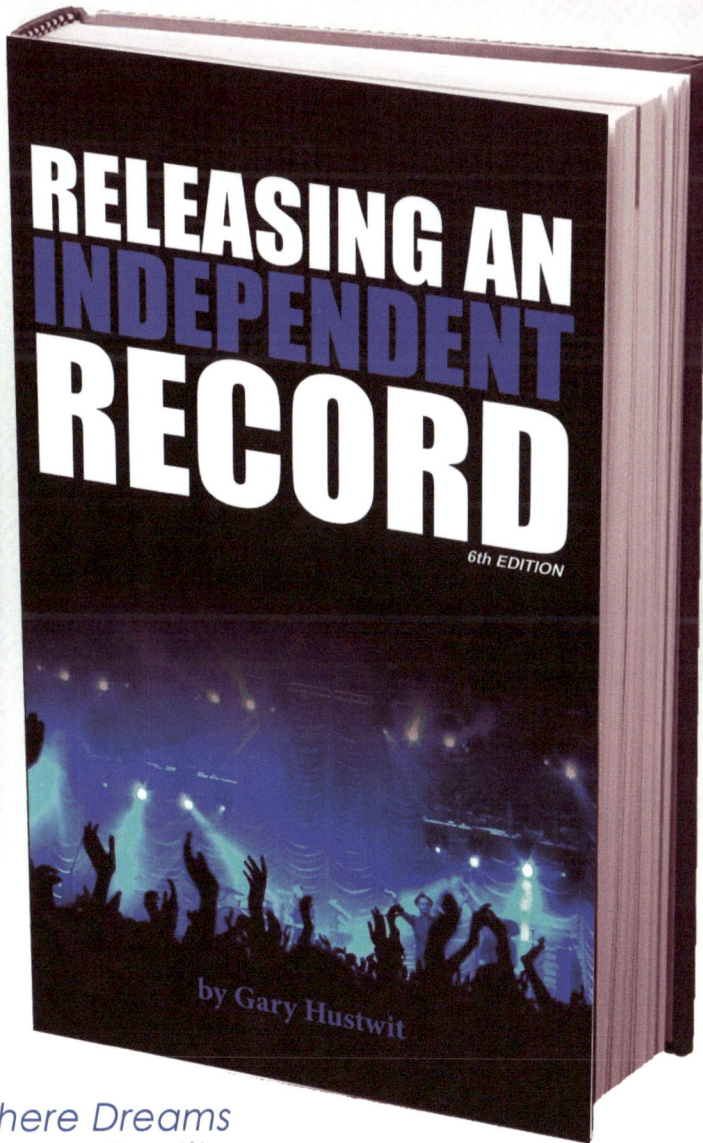

THE ALL NEW STYLE OF MAGAZINE-BOOKS

SDM LIVE®

www.ingramcontent.com/pod-product-compliance
Lightning Source LLC
Chambersburg PA
CBHW041527070426

42452CB00036B/33